Red Bank

David Annwn

NEWTON-LE-WILLOWS

Published in the United Kingdom in 2018
by The Knives Forks And Spoons Press,
51 Pipit Avenue,
Newton-le-Willows,
Merseyside,
WA12 9RG.

ISBN 978-1-912211-19-7

Copyright © David Annwn, 2018.

The right of David Annwn to be identified as the author of this work has been asserted by them in accordance with the Copyrights, Designs and Patents Act of 1988. All rights reserved. No part of this publication may be reproduced, stored in a retrieval system, transmitted in any form or by any means, electronic, photocopying, recording or otherwise, without prior permission of the publisher.

Acknowledgements:

Red Bank

TABLE OF CONTENTS

Red Bank	9
The last Masque	25
Harvest	41

I

Red Bank

      cymbals hissing
as if there's something
going on underneath
'Penny Lane' finishing

and a piccolo trumpet, sparrow trill
McCartney's jaunt
borrowed from Brandenberg

a nurse offering poppies
fish, chips and the Queen,
the lane's name borrowed from slavery.

Lennon's 'Jesus' in that same year
more than 50 years ago – so soon.
Times by seven and you're back

on Red Bank with Royalists
running, shouting "Mercy Mercy"
echoeing five miles away.

raising the ordinary
to holy, the mysterious
and working class to Baroque

concerto royal – a tripping
and walking rhythm
their tasks suddenly surreal
and strange.

Anyone is free to Hermitage Green Lane.

David Annwn

McCartney's 'Golden Slumbers' borrowed
from Thomas Dekker, words
written 50 years before
men ran the field at Red Bank:

once we knew a way
to go back, for McCartney
to his mother's home

for us to walk in the door
to parents, a sister, two brothers.

Red Bank

Cromwell's fenland grey-green eyes
weighed this incline
came as silent suns to night.

Too much of it lost
under work and study though we hid
on the bank with our willow-herb spears.

Red Bank assessment unit
for young offenders – once we knew
a way – kept them fit

and away from their families.
Their dormitories backed our
bungalow road; each mode

and splay of their sleeping minds
precious – though not a *screw*
I was a screw's son.

A dentist, a doctor's, a Baths
and our own Pictures and Hammer's 'Curse
of the Mummy's Tomb'.

Mary, infamous voice called out
through concrete bars and glass,
she said "Come and talk to me."

Greensward and running track at my
back, embankment and power cable
buzzing the line to Liverpool.

"If there were just the two of us
we could go away; what do you
think about – to somewhere special"

and, a few weeks later: "I didn't do
it you know" – but I knew
she did, under the sign of the

falling child. Not Karloff or Christopher
Lee or a shambling mummy
or an amputated hand which haunted me.

Mary, Mary, quite contrary?
Palest blue eyes and a style
of clothes too old for style
and a Geordie accent
waiting for afternoons of years:
"Come and talk to me."

David Annwn

We pursued to Warrington Bridge, which
the Scots kept till our body came up. It
is wonderful to see how many are slaine all
the way […] from Wigan to Warrington, all
the high ways, Corne Fields, Meddows, Woods
and ditches strewed with dead bodies.

Red Bank

and Red Bank no place
for children to play, a battlefield,
1600 in a grave unmarked,

trees, with bark autographed
by the RAF 1941 and their lovers,
soared and wheeled their freight:

ferns, glades and heights above the brook
two adolescents, one's shirt frilled
á la Jason King, and moustached

two adders twining on tussocks
of sharp grass; anyone is free
piccolo trumpet and sparrows
as though there's something going on.

so played out – it burgeoned stasis
a place to project otherwheres from:
San Francisco, London

Boys and girls tumbling
were moving jewels
but I couldn't get to them.

There are times in a living person
that I see such love and passion
it awes so much I'm frightened
It breaks out, and I see through to somewhere
else outside the rhythm of headlines
bold type of confused malevolence
illness and want; there are those
whose daily condition is to labour
for the good and relief, which does
not mean they are unshaded or marred
but that it comes to them seemingly
as natural as water. Like a door
unopened we have forgotten
in the annals of recorded time.

the bungalow is under grass
that door gone; yet the boys
and girl have gone on into
their lives, (where else?)
encouraged in skill, to
fend off harm, to be together
when they can.

The Red Bank cliff a conduit
between suburbia and farm.

II

The last Masque

A tripping gait gathering
impetus in the air: 'Get back'
on this blustery rooftop: 69
shouting sheer drop
over Georgian facades
to Savile Row

Canter and strum, sashay
with intricate picking
almost whinnying, softly
whining, gathering to
the reining in
the block and power
of double chording, P90 tone
of Lennon's sanded-down
Epiphone Casino.

The Beatles' last
concert, as a crowd
laid wreaths on Charing
Cross island, look. Across
Piccadilly and St James's
to the Whitehall site

of the King's scaffold
and banqueting hall.

David Annwn

Go home to your last resting place,
to Renfrew, to Linlithgow
you levied and rain-sodden, you
called-up cursed darlings
and stew-frequenters and those of you
who longed to go strung out
on baggage abandoned with songs
and lust and drookit mornings.
Go home admonished.
No, Cromwell will deny you
any than homeless gloaming
and winnowed into the stubblefield.

The habit of his Majesty:
aquamarine embroidered
with silver, long stockings
of white, caps silver

with plumes of white:
'All that are harsh, all that are rude
Are by your harmony subdued'.
The king is dancing dominion

over land and courtiers.
In nine years will pass
through casement here
to Theatrum tragicum
his black-clothed stage.

He will dance from Inigo
Jones's sketched: 'cornfields
and pleasant trees', a valley,
past Cromwell's horsemen
hacking Berwick men
over Redbank edge.

If you wake in the middle night
play Anna Dennis singing
Robert Herrick's 'Gather ye rosebuds
while ye may', from 1648
with William Lawes' lunar music
remote and incontestable,
those vast distances, and the
drone of the viol, and the haunting fall
warning virgins not to tarry
inviolable as angels.

To read these fields by the king's
festivities, a reinvention
and self-fashioning.

As in the habit of masquerade
Sgt Pepper's reflective wit
uniforms conscripted

ornately anti-
establishment. Even Hendrix
ex-paratrooper
in his black hussar's jacket.

Once on the corner of North Parade
and Terrace Road, his cortège pulling
level without foreknowledge or
outriding blazon, and for a second,
he and I were alone together you
know in all the wide world, eye to eye
through limousine glass, soul to soul,
object and subject, and he waved at
me but I stared him outright with
what was imagined as indifferent coldness
and would not wave back

Carolus Hic Rexque Futurus.

David Annwn

For the boys at the school
and the masters with meal-
time discipline
a throwback to the army
with assessing address:
Dixon, Miles and my father
with severe eye and warming,
did they believe the concrete
rested easy under them, only
two decades on from war;
for those on night duty
in the dormitories?

Red Bank

This is your scape for young
offenders, for a teenager
listening to Mary more desperately
as you walk the track:
"Come and talk with me, Come" and
"…What do you do in this place? Who
is your father, your sister? What
do you think?" You're warned away
told sternly off from concrete slits.

Hermet-
        ically
sealed it was not, this
harboured convocation on the edge
invested in redemption – even the Closed Unit
had visitors. Sometimes we searched
for the hermit by the well
in Hermitage
Green Lane.

this war, this farce, this masque
with musket-shot and smoke miasma
this slogged terrain with rain-flattened corn
these drenched albeit starving men
harvested by raveners
I read these fields by the king's festivities.

David Annwn

In the promo for Penny Lane
in red hunting jackets,
riding white horses under
the arch at Royalist Knole
as in Van Dyck's oil:
'Charles 1 with M. de St Antoine';
The king's last masque
mocked alchemists and seers
who offered for the physic
of this 'over-lucky, too-much-happy isle'
uncouth remedies
when those tricked up as gods
'celestial prospect, with chorus below'
could see no further than their noses.

Britain was made and unmade
on this field we thought then marginal
as ourselves:
in fealty to the mystery of fields.

III

Harvest

A harpsichord prelude
    slowly-stepped
      descent into spell
     a pavane with
       triple tempi for chorus

Lucy's in the sky with diamonds
again and so is the queen:
'a huge cloud of various colours
and within a transparent brightness
of thin exhalations, such as the gods
are feigned to descend in'
"We're more popular than Jesus"
'from over her head dart
lightsome rays.'

David Annwn

The lane is close in, cliff high on
first entrance, then right a lay-by
a driveway, a surge of tall trees,
the bend that follows initiates
the wood spreading our places

James Marquis Hamilton
danced with the Prince Charles in Jonson's
masque, in white and crimson
with darkened masks:
Thirty years later, Hamilton's son
leaving his men's flank
spurred away from Red Bank
abandoning his Lanarkshires
to the favours
of Twizelton's riders
and no-nonsense Sanderson.

David Annwn

Nine days after the massacre
'Upon my reaping Day the
28th of August 1648'
writes Mildmay Fane
of Westmorland, a nobleman:
'But every one in their Compartments Come
And reape and binde and loade my Hock Cart home'
in imitation of Herrick's idyll
which was a mode of dealing
denial
to the bulked ruck
of fallen men
what harvest-home?

Three men over Redbank ride:
Lilburne, Cromwell and Thomas Pride,
Each signed the charter for regicide,
The brook ran red from Whitehall's side.

David Annwn

It is another England

streaming backwards over
psychedelic plains
of 70s Lancashire
through grey corridors
and bus terminals
to (where else)
Carroll's church at Daresbury
not far as you might think
as the raven flies
-triple tempi for chorus-
where Lennon caught a walrus.

Red Bank

below the grass cliff's platform
seed-heads incredibly high
shouldering temptation
to fly-tippers,
pastures opening left
and right
as you pass the farms'
perspectival
horses

David Annwn

Westwards, there's a burnt-out
Fiesta on the cindertrack
below Cop Holt wood.

To have seen seasonally the farm bonfire
with its acrid toffee and raked potatoes
and a calf, with sacs pulled around it,
born
and Fawkes's effigy flare
and stranger things
flicker
a schoolscape lasting one hundred and fifty
years vanish
to walk the track
and then forget
the sleeve

Requiescat in pace

Where is the well's hermit
of this green Hermitage?

www.ingramcontent.com/pod-product-compliance
Lightning Source LLC
Chambersburg PA
CBHW032103040426
42449CB00007B/1172